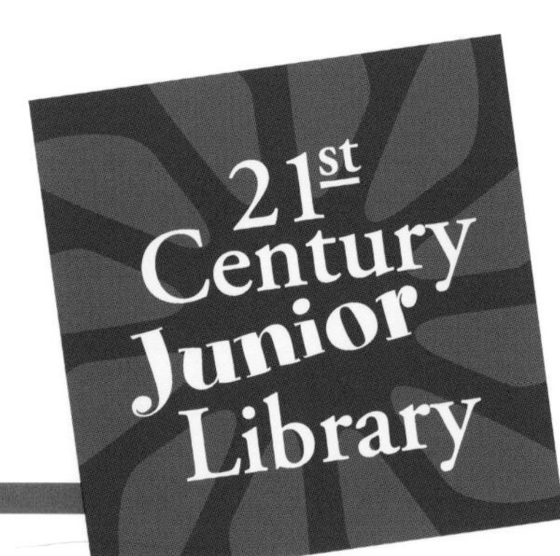

WORKING AT A MOVIE THEATER

by Susan Hindman

CHERRY LAKE PUBLISHING * ANN ARBOR, MICHIGAN

Published in the United States of America by Cherry Lake Publishing
Ann Arbor, Michigan
www.cherrylakepublishing.com

Content Adviser: Michael Lefebvre, Director of Operations, Ragtag Cinema
Reading Adviser: Cecilia Minden-Cupp, PhD, Literacy Consultant

Photo Credits: Cover, ©iStockphoto.com/Nnehring and ©iStockphoto.com/asiseeit; cover and page 10, ©Sparky2000/Dreamstime.com; cover and page 12, ©Rramirez125/Dreamstime.com; page 4, ©Frances M. Roberts/Alamy; pages 6 and 20, ©Jeff Greenberg/Alamy; page 8, ©iStockphoto.com/LeggNet; page 14, ©67photo/Alamy; page 16, ©iStockphoto.com/withgod; page 18, ©i love images/Alamy

LIBRARY OF CONGRESS CATALOGING-IN-PUBLICATION DATA

Hindman, Susan.
Working at a movie theater/by Susan Hindman.
p. cm.—(21st century junior library)
Includes bibliographical references and index.
ISBN-13: 978-1-60279-979-0 (lib. bdg.)
ISBN-10: 1-60279-979-2 (lib. bdg.)
1. Motion picture theaters—Employees—Juvenile literature. 2. Motion picture industry—Employees—Juvenile literature. I. Title. II. Series.
PN1994.5.H497 2011
725'.823023—dc22 2010029758

Cherry Lake Publishing would like to acknowledge the work of The Partnership for 21st Century Skills.
Please visit www.21stcenturyskills.org *for more information.*

Printed in the United States of America
Corporate Graphics Inc.
January 2011
CLSP08

CONTENTS

Movie theaters are exciting places.

What Is a Movie Theater?

Look at the colorful lights on that building! There are so many cars in the parking lot. A big sign lists the names of movies. People are standing in line to buy tickets. Where are you? You are at a movie theater!

Some movie theaters are very big.

Inside the theater is the **lobby**. Big posters are on the walls. They have pictures of movie stars on them. TV screens show movie **trailers**.

The lobby is noisy. The smell of popcorn makes you hungry.

Many people enjoy watching movies.

Most theaters show more than one movie. The biggest movie theaters have as many as 30 **screens**. How will you find the movie you want to see? Where will you sit? You have many questions. Workers at the movie theater can answer them.

How many people go to the movies? It depends on the day of the week. It also depends on where you live. Do you think more people go on a weekday or a weekend? Remember that new movies often start playing on Fridays.

Cashiers work in the box office. That's the part of the theater where tickets are sold.

Movie Theater Workers

You decide which movie you want to see. Next you give your money to the **cashier**. She gives you a ticket. She can answer questions about the movie. She can tell you its **rating** and how long it is.

There are many treats to choose from at the concession stand.

You decide you want something to eat and drink. You walk up to the **concession stand**. The worker there can help you pick out a treat. You might choose candy, soda, or popcorn. Some theaters have special treats for children.

Look at all that popcorn! How is it made? It's easy! Workers pour popcorn seeds into the machine. Then they add salt and oil and close the lid. The popcorn is ready in less than 5 minutes.

The projectionist needs to know how to work the movie equipment.

The **usher** takes your ticket. You walk into the crowded theater and sit down. The lights go down. The screen gets bright.

You look behind you. There is a light coming from a small window. The **projectionist** works there. He sets up the movie and makes sure there are no problems.

The cleaning crew makes sure the seats and floor are clean for the next day.

The last movie of the day has ended. Now the **cleaning crew** comes in. They clean up the trash.

Managers make sure everything goes smoothly. They hire workers. They help teach workers how to do their jobs. The general manager is in charge of everything. He makes sure the other managers do their jobs.

Most movie theaters are owned by big companies. Some are owned by one person or a few people. The owners get to choose what movies to show. What if you owned a movie theater? What kinds of movies would you choose?

Movie theater workers usually wear uniforms.

Do You Want to Work at a Movie Theater?

You can work at a movie theater when you are in high school. You could be a ticket seller, concession stand worker, or usher. Projectionists need to know how to use the machines that play the films. Managers need experience. They have to work in movie theaters for a few years.

Look for different workers the next time you visit the movie theater!

Do you like movies? Do you enjoy working with other people? Then you might want a job at a movie theater. Working at a movie theater can be a lot of fun!

What is the best thing about working at a movie theater? What is the hardest thing? Ask a theater worker to find out the answers!

GLOSSARY

cashier (ka-SHIHR) someone who takes money and gives change in a theater or store

cleaning crew (KLEEN-ing KROO) people who work together to clean a theater or other place

concession stand (kun-SESH-uhn STAND) a place where theater workers sell soda, popcorn, candy, and other snacks

lobby (LAH-bee) a large room at the entrance of a theater or other building

managers (MA-nih-jurz) people who are in charge of a business or a group of workers

projectionist (pruh-JEK-shun-ist) the person who shows the movies on a screen

rating (RAYT-ing) a grade that says how old you should be to see a certain movie

screens (SKREENZ) the large, flat surfaces where movies are shown

trailers (TRAY-lurz) very short films that show parts of new movies

usher (UH-shur) someone who takes tickets and shows people where to sit in a theater

FIND OUT MORE

BOOKS

Lyons, Shelly, and Ronnie Rooney (illustrator). *If I Were a Movie Star.* Mankato, MN: Picture Window Books, 2010.

Meinking, Mary. *Who Rolls Through Fire? Working on a Movie Set.* Chicago: Raintree, 2010.

WEB SITES

AMC Entertainment: Theatre Crew
www.amcentertainment.com/amcinfo/careers/theatre_crew/
Learn about different jobs at movie theaters.

Drive-In Theater
www.driveintheater.com/
Visit this site to learn more about drive-in movie theaters.

INDEX

ABOUT THE AUTHOR

Susan Hindman is a freelance editor and writer in Colorado Springs. She has two college-age daughters. She took them to movies all the time when they were young. Susan would like to thank Hollywood Theaters for help with her research.